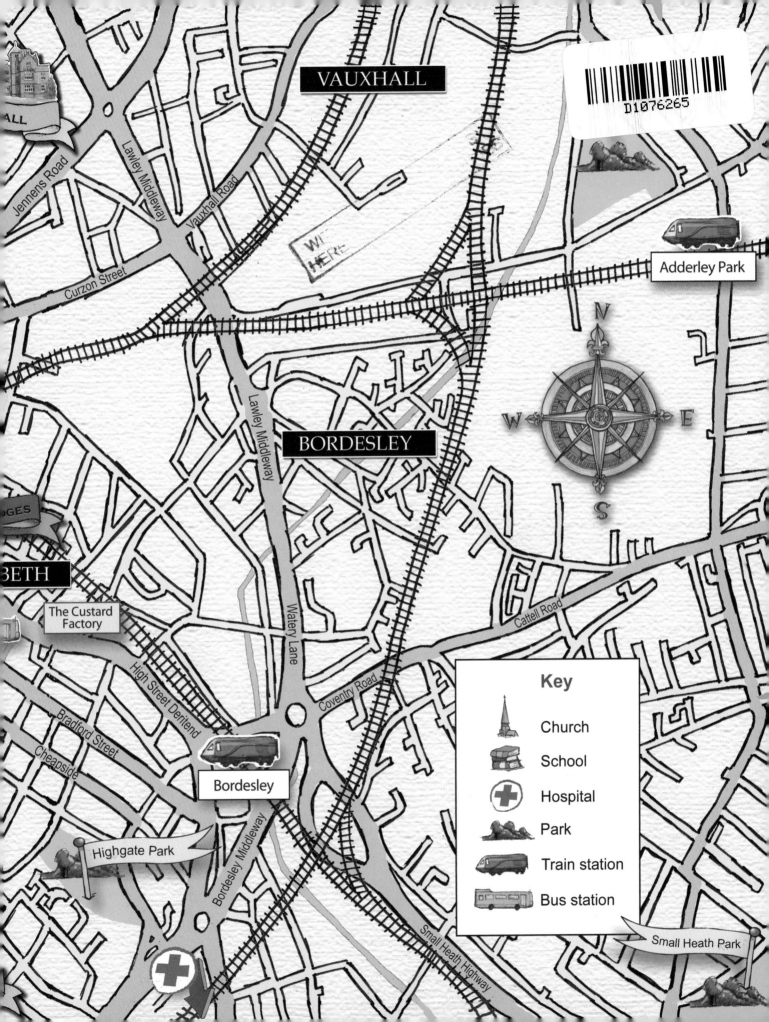

children's HISTORY of BIRMINGHAM

Written by
Mandy Ross

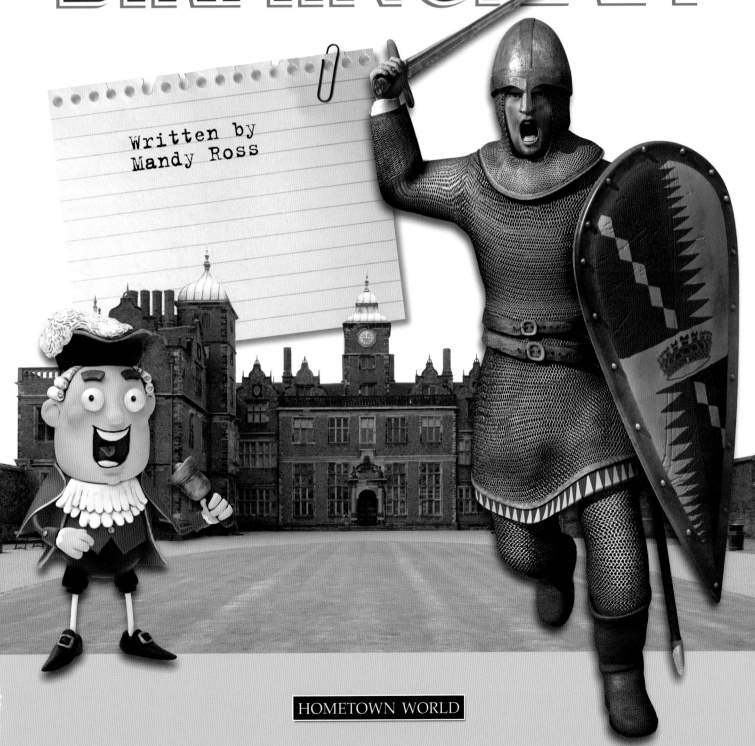

HOMETOWN WORLD

How well do you know your town?

Have you ever wondered what it would have been like living in Birmingham when the Romans arrived? What about swapping ideas with the best brains in Britain at Soho House? This book will uncover the important and exciting things that happened in your town.

Want to hear the other good bits? You will love this book! Some rather brainy folk have worked on it to make sure it's fun and informative. So what are you waiting for? Peel back the pages and be amazed at what happened in Birmingham.

THE FACTS

Timeline shows which period (dates and people) each spread is talking about

Clear informative text

Hometown facts to amaze you!

'Spot this!' game with hints on something to find in your town

THE EVIDENCE

Go back in time to read what it was like for children growing up in Birmingham

Each period in the book ends with a summary explaining how we know about the past

Intriguing old pictures

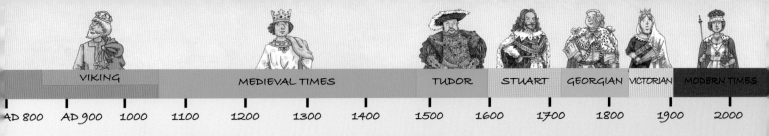

Contents

The Romans are Here!

The straight, paved road runs through deep forest. Roman soldiers march briskly outside the fort as the sun sets behind the trees. Messengers in speedy two-wheeled chariots try to overtake the slow, heavy haycart. A boy drives his honking geese into the thatched wooden village next to the fort. Everyone hurries to get safely back home before dark.

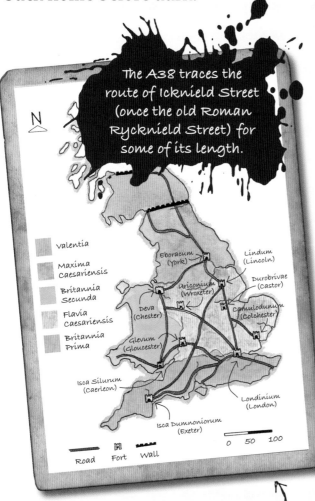

The A38 traces the route of Icknield Street (once the old Roman Rycknield Street) for some of its length.

This map shows the main areas, roads and forts in Roman Britain about AD 43.

Why Britain?

That's Rycknield Street finished - should last another 2,000 years!

The Romans arrived in Britain in about AD 43. The Celtic people living in the Birmingham area lived in deep forest. But beneath the trees lay valuable minerals such as coal and iron. And that was what the Romans wanted. Some Britons welcomed the Romans, but not all the tribes were happy.

The mighty Roman army swiftly conquered most of England and Wales. Within just a few years, working at an amazing pace, highly-trained Roman soldiers built a network of roads criss-crossing most of the country. Roman roads were very straight, cutting through Britain's dense forests.

TUDOR
1485-1603

STUART
1603-1714

GEORGIAN
1714-1837

VICTORIAN
1837-1901

MODERN TIMES
1902-NOW

Birmingham's Roman Fort

Metchley Fort was built in about AD 48, where Birmingham University is now. It stood near a junction on Icknield Street, a Roman road. The road linked Wall (near Lichfield) to Alcester and Droitwich.

The fort was built of wood, surrounded by a double ditch and high fence. A thousand soldiers could live inside. It must have been crowded and noisy. There were workshops, kitchens, store-rooms, bathrooms... and shared toilets seating several men in a row!

Some British tribes lived peacefully alongside the Romans – as long as they paid the Roman taxes. A small British village grew up nestling beside the walls of Metchley Fort.

What shall we call this fort then?

Plan of Metchley Fort

—— Double ditch

===== Road

N

Original fort

Areas added to original fort

Smaller fort built later

Local settlement

0 m   100 m

Metchley Fort was about the size of 4 football pitches.

I've learned to bake soft white bread like the Romans.

How do we know?

We don't know what the Romans called their fort here in Birmingham. Metchley is a name from a later time. Over the last 80 years, archaeologists have carefully dug up parts of Metchley Fort. They have found cooking pots made in the Malverns, fine tableware from France, and fragments of glass cups and bowls. This tells us a little about life in the fort.

SPOT THIS!
Can you spot the old Roman Rycknield Street in Sutton Park?

...AD 48 METCHLEY FORT BUILT...ABOUT AD 410 ROMANS LEAVE BIRMINGHAM...

5

Beorma's People

Chop! Chop! Chop! Axes echo through the dense forest beside the river crossing. At last, a warning shout: 'Timber!' The men watch as the huge oak tree crashes to the ground. By the river, women and children have been cutting back the undergrowth to clear the ground. It is hard and weary work. But soon the new field will be ready for planting.

A Saxon home was built of wood with a roof thatched with straw. There was just one room inside with a cooking pot over a fire in the centre.

Birmingham's Beginnings

The Anglo-Saxon village was growing. The villagers needed extra fields to grow more food. A small band of settlers had chosen this spot at the crossing-place of the small River Rea back in the 7th century AD. They had come from northern Europe in search of land for farming. The name 'Birmingham' comes from an Anglo-Saxon name, Beorma-ing-ham – which means 'the village of Beorma's people'. (And that's why you are now called a Brummie!)

The people worked together to clear woodland to make big, open fields. Each family had a strip of the field to grow wheat, peas or beans. Some kept sheep or a cow, or bees for honey. As soon as they could, the children worked in the fields.

Oh! My back's killing me!

These oxen pulling a plough are pictured in an 11th century manuscript.

...AD 600s BEORMA'S PEOPLE SETTLE BY RIVER REA...

Pagans and Christians

King Penda ruled Mercia, the midlands kingdom, until AD 655. Penda followed the old pagan religion, worshipping gods from nature. Perhaps the gold dug up recently in the Mercian hoard belonged to someone like him.

Christianity spread quickly in the 7th and 8th centuries. The Anglo-Saxons began to build churches using stone. A churchman called Chad helped to bring Christianity to Mercia. Today, St Chad's Catholic Cathedral is named after him.

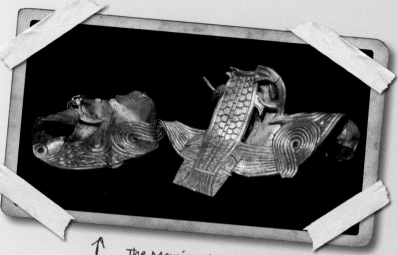

The Mercian hoard of Saxon gold was found in 2009, buried on farmland in Staffordshire not far from Birmingham.

Who is this Beorma? No one knows for sure!

Birmingham has no Viking place names. This tells us the Vikings never settled around Birmingham.

How do we know?

Most of Birmingham's place names come from Anglo-Saxon words. This tells us that many local settlements were started in Anglo-Saxon times.

Lots of Birmingham place names end with -ley, such as Moseley and Yardley. This comes from 'leah', Anglo-Saxon for 'a clearing in woodland'. Can you find other Birmingham place names ending with -ley?

The spelling of 'Birmingham' has changed over time. How many different spellings can you count in this book?

SPOT THIS!

This bridge marks the crossing point of the River Rea where Birmingham began.

...AD 655 KING PENDA OF MERCIA DIES...AD 672 ST CHAD DIES...

7

CELT
500 BC

ROMAN
AD 43-410

ANGLO-
SAXON
AD 450-
1066

VIKING
AD 865-
1066

MEDIEVAL
TIMES
1066-148!

The Bull Ring

Ding… ding… ding! St Martin's Church bells ring over the din of Birmingham's famous Bull Ring Market. Traders shout their wares at stalls crowded between the wooden houses. Pigs, sheep and cows bellow and stamp in the mud at the Beast Market. Usually the market is busy. But this week there are only a few customers. Rumours of the plague are keeping them away!

The 'Bull Ring' was a bull-baiting enclosure started by a man called John Cooper in the 1500s.

The tomb of Sir William de Birmingham in St Martin's Church, dating from 1325, is the oldest monument in the city.

Backwater to Busy Market Town

Back in 1086, Birmingham was a poor manor with just 50 people. In the following century, the lord of the manor, Peter de Birmingham, wanted to make Birmingham great. But how? It had neither rich farmland nor a sea-port. So, in 1166, Peter bought a royal charter, which allowed him to hold a weekly market.

Soon the market was thriving. Every Thursday, farmers brought their crops and animals to the Bull Ring Market. Craft workers from Digbeth sold woollen cloth, knives, iron nails and horse shoes. There were costly luxuries like paper, soap – and even spices and oranges from faraway lands. Farmers from as far away as north Wales drove their herds of sheep and cattle to the Welsh End of the market between Dale End and Bull Street.

Chew this. It might not work but it'll help take your mind off the scabs.

Fire and Plague

Word spread about the Bull Ring Market. Merchants and craft workers came to live nearby. But there were disasters in store. The Great Fire of Birmingham was recorded in 1313. Two years later, terrible rains and poor harvests brought the Great Famine. And, worst of all, in 1349 – plague! Half or more of Birmingham's people died.

 SPOT THIS!

The Old Crown, built around 1450, is the oldest inn in central Birmingham. It has been a guild hall, school and slaughterhouse. Today it is an inn again.

The original market charter allowed a market to be held every Thursday at Birmingham 'Castle'. This was later changed to Birmingham 'township'.

I've walked all the way from Wales. I hope someone buys me so I don't have to walk home again!

How do we know?

This is part of the market charter granted by King Henry II.

1166

Henry II, King of England, to all his faithful of all England, greetings.

Know that I have granted to the Lord of Dudley (Peter de Birmingham) and to his heirs that he may have a market on Thursdays at his Castle of Burmingeham.

In 1086, the manor of Birmingham was worth 20 shillings according to the Domesday Book.

CELT
500 BC

ROMAN
AD 43-410

ANGLO-
SAXON
AD 450-
1066

VIKING
AD 865-
1066

MEDIEVAL
TIMES
1066-
1485

Weapons and War

It is the night before battle. At Aston Hall, Royalist forces have gathered. Down in the town, the men are getting ready to fight them. Birmingham supports the Parliamentarians. Lads help their fathers to oil muskets proudly forged in Birmingham. Weeping women have kissed their sons and husbands goodbye, not knowing if they will see them alive again. Tonight they must pray before they sleep.

Metal Workers

Tudor Birmingham had become famous for its skilled metal-workers. Blacksmiths made all sorts of metal goods, including swords, chains and locks. Water mills, like Sarehole Mill on the River Cole, turned grindstones for rolling metal. Do you know anyone whose surname is Cutler, Nailor or Smith? Their ancestors were probably metal-workers. Cutlers made knives, nailors made nails, and blacksmiths hammered iron on their anvils. By this time its metal-workers were making guns, cannonballs and ammunition. When the English Civil War began, Birmingham's gun makers were busier than ever.

By the end of the 17th century, Birmingham was making over 200 muskets a month.

Civil War

The English Civil War started when King Charles I quarrelled with his Parliament in 1642. Birmingham sided strongly with the Parliamentarians against the king. The Parliamentarians fought using Birmingham's muskets and ammunition.

Musketeers carried guns called matchlocks. They didn't shoot very straight and were tricky to reload quickly during battle.

TUDOR
1485-1603

STUART
1603-1714

GEORGIAN
1714-1837

VICTORIAN
1837-1901

MODERN
TIMES
1902-NOW

Aston Hall

At Aston Hall, however, Sir Thomas Holte supported King Charles. During 1642, Charles I spent a night at Aston Hall on his way to battle at Edgehill. The king's nephew, Prince Rupert, was on his way to meet the king when he was caught up in a battle on Kings Norton Green. He was outnumbered by the Parliamentarians and retreated.

In 1643, Prince Rupert once again led Royalist troops in the Battle of Camp Hill (sometimes called the Battle of Birmingham). A small band of Birmingham Parliamentarians held them back firing muskets. But Prince Rupert split up his forces and attacked the town from two sides. At last, the Parliamentarians withdrew and Prince Rupert won. His troops rode through the town and set light to the houses. The attack became known as the 'Birmingham Butcheries'.

The following year, Sir Thomas set up a garrison at Aston Hall with 40 musketeers sent from Dudley. By Christmas the hall was under seige and being bombarded by cannonfire. Sir Thomas was forced to surrender.

There is a hole in the staircase at Aston Hall where a cannonball hit.

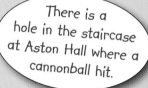

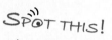

SPOT THIS!

This plaque above Aston Hall tells us exactly when it was built. It took 17 years to complete!

How do we know?

The Parliamentarians wrote this account of the 'Birmingham Butcheries'. Can we rely on it being accurate?

True Relation of Prince Rupert's Barbarous Cruelty against the Town of Brumingham. To which place on Monday 3 April 1643, he marched with 2000 horse and foot soldiers; where after two hours fight (being twice beaten off by the Townsmen, in all but 140 Musketeers) he entered, put many to the Sword, and burnt about 80 Houses to ashes, suffering no man to carry away his goods, or quench the fire.

By 1646, King Charles I was defeated. He was tried for treason and beheaded in 1649.

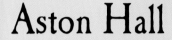

Machines and Manufacturing

As the evening sun sets behind Soho House, with its grand columns and beautiful gardens, the carriages start to arrive. Industrialist Matthew Boulton welcomes his guests for tonight's Lunar Society meeting – some of the sharpest brains in Britain. Tonight Scottish engineer James Watt will present plans for his powerful new steam engine. Ideas fly around the table until past midnight. There are no streetlights, but the bright moon lights the members safely home.

James Watt gave his name to the Watt, the unit of electrical energy.

Handmade – or Machine-made?

A gilded statue of Boulton, Watt and Murdoch stands on Broad Street. It was made by William Bloye in 1956.

Birmingham's Lunar Society met from 1765 – always on the night of the full moon. That is why its members were known as the 'Lunaticks'! It brought together great engineers, scientists, businessmen and inventors.

Eighteenth century Birmingham rang with the sound of thousands of hammers of skilled metal-workers in small workshops. Many children and young people worked with them, to earn money so their families could eat.

The Lunaticks set about using science to make manufacturing easier and quicker. They built factories and invented huge, powerful machines which could do the work of many people.

News of the Lunar Society spread far and wide. William Murdoch was a young Scottish engineer and inventor. In 1777, he walked 480 km to Birmingham to ask for a job with Boulton and Watt. They took him on!

...1765 LUNAR SOCIETY MEETS...1772 BIRMINGHAM CANAL BUILT...

Canals

Two rival companies built the canals that today meet at Gas Street Basin.

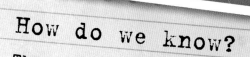

Britain's roads were terrible, especially in winter. Transporting Birmingham's metal goods was slow, difficult and expensive. The canals changed all that. James Brindley, one of the Lunaticks, built Birmingham's first canal in 1772.

Soon more canals criss-crossed Birmingham than Venice! Birmingham's metal goods were loaded onto barges and carried across the country.

Spot this!

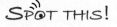

Can you spot this statue of Thomas Atwood, Birmingham's first Member of Parliament in 1832? Clue: check the steps in Chamberlain Square.

The Slave Trade

The metal trade had a grimmer side too. Birmingham's chains, padlocks and guns were used in the slave trade. They imprisoned African people taken as slaves to the Caribbean.

But many people in Birmingham wanted to end slavery. Olaudah Equiano was a freed slave. He campaigned to end slavery. In 1790, Equiano visited Birmingham to spread the word. From 1825 the Female Society for Birmingham called for a speedy end to slavery. Slavery was banned at last in 1833.

How do we know?

This is how the writer Arthur Young described Birmingham, which he visited in 1791.

The capital improvement since I was here before is the canal; the port in the town crowded with coal barges is a noble spectacle. I looked around me with amazement at the change effected in twelve years; this place may now probably be reckoned the first manufacturing town in the world. From this port you may now go by water to Hull, Liverpool, Bristol, Oxford and London.

This portrait of Equiano appears in 'The Interesting Narrative of the Life of Olaudah Equiano, or Gustavus Vassa, the African', published in 1789.

CELT   500 BC

ROMAN AD 43-410

ANGLO-SAXON AD 450-1066

VIKING AD 865-1066

MEDIEVAL TIMES
1066-1485

Workshop of the World

The gas lights are still lit over the dark streets. Horse-drawn carts rattle over the cobbles. But today the dawn streets are crowded. At seven o'clock precisely, the steam train puffs slowly out of Birmingham's Curzon Street Station. Faster and faster, it reaches the dizzying speed of 30 miles an hour! The watching crowds cheer and wave their hats and handkerchiefs.

Peep! What a daft place to have a picnic!

The railway passed by Aston Hall in 1851.

Railway Mania!

The railway boom had begun! Birmingham's first railway linked the city to Manchester and Liverpool. In the years after Victoria became queen in 1837, railway lines were networking across the country.

Victorian Birmingham was called the 'city of a thousand trades'. It manufactured anything from guns to pens. The new railways carried manufactured goods out of Birmingham much faster than the canals.

During Victoria's reign, England ruled many other countries, called the colonies. British manufacturers could buy goods cheaply from the colonies, such as sugar from the Caribbean, cocoa from West Africa, and gold from South Africa. This helped Birmingham's industries, such as Bird's Custard, Cadbury's chocolate and the jewellery trade.

 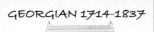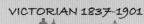 
Settling In

Victorian Birmingham was growing fast. People flocked to the city to work in the factories. Many came from Ireland after the terrible famine there in 1846. A Jewish community grew up from Germany, Russia and Poland. By the 1860s, Birmingham's population was a quarter of a million. The streets must have been full of different accents!

Workshop owners made huge profits and skilled workers earned good wages. But millions of men, women and children working long hours were desperately poor. In the slums most people lived in terrible conditions. Rat-infested houses were crowded together, with many families sharing a water-pump and a toilet. A whole family might live in just a single room or even a cellar. Many went hungry. Drinking water was often unclean. Sewage ran through the streets (imagine the smell!). Dangerous diseases spread in these dirty conditions.

I caw run 'ome, I 'ent got boots like yow!

In the 19th century, Birmingham claimed that 75% of everything written in the world was with a 'Birmingham pen'!

The new Birmingham Workhouse opened in 1852. Today Birmingham City Hospital stands on the same site.

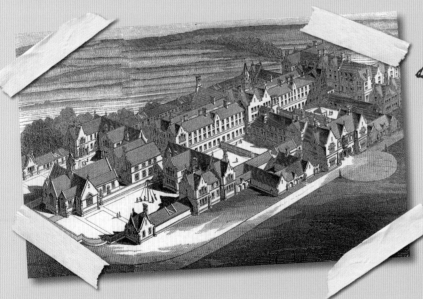

The Arch of Tears

In Victorian Britain, if you could not work to earn money, you and your family would starve. The very poorest had no choice but to go into the workhouse. It was very shameful, called going through the 'arch of tears'. Families were split up as men, women and children lived in different sections. The food was dreadful and life was very grim.

Many children died before they had a chance to grow up.

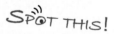

SPOT THIS!

Can you spot this plaque on the old Curzon Street Station? It tells you the exact date of the first ever train from London to Birmingham.

CURZON STREET STATION

THIS PLAQUE COMMEMORATES THE 150TH ANNIVERSARY OF THE ARRIVAL OF THE FIRST LONDON TO BIRMINGHAM TRAIN AT THIS STATION ON MONDAY 17TH SEPTEMBER 1838.

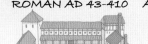

Here is a made-up account from Rose Cutler, aged 10, on entering the Birmingham Workhouse on 7th November 1854 with her mother and younger brothers.

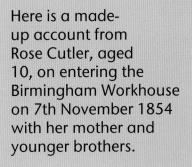

> I hope we don't get split up.

> I'm hungry!

When Father was alive, he worked in the Bird's Custard Factory in Digbeth. Once he brought us home a taste of the custard. I can still remember the sweetness.

But he died last year from the cholera, and then my sister Ellen too. They say it was from drinking dirty water, but what else can we drink? The pump in our courtyard brings water from the River Rea. You can see with your own eyes how dirty it is.

Mother and I have tried so hard to keep us together. But it's no good. She can't work since her accident at the factory three years ago. And my wages are very little, even though I work 12 hours a day. The littl'uns are cold and hungry every night. We have no choice but to come here, even though it means we might be apart...

NAME	RELATION	CONDITION	AGE	OCCUPATION	WHERE BORN	DISABILITY
John Condrey	Inmate	Unm	56	Gardener	Edgbaston,WAR	Has fits
Charles Wilkins	Inmate	Unm	23	Shoemaker	Birmingham,WAR	Has fits
William Atkins	Inmate	Unm	35	Idiot	Handsworth,STS	Idiot from birth
Thomas Johnson	Inmate	Unm	66	Idiot	Bednell,WOR	Idiot from birth + Cripple
Sarah Taylor	Inmate	Widow	73	None	Not known	
Sarah Green	Inmate	Unm	25	Servant	Birmingham,WAR	
Ellen Serivens	Inmate	Unm	14		Edgbaston,WAR	Deaf & dumb since ??
Ellen Pleavin	Inmate	Unm	31	Servant	Cheshire,CHE	
John Grigg	Inmate	Child	13	None	Unknown	
William Grigg	Inmate	Child	11	None	Unknow	
Joseph Grigg	Inmate	Child	8	None	Unknown	
Thomas ??	Inmate	Child	8	None	Unknown	

This is an extract from Kings Norton Workhouse Census 1871. 'Unm' is short for 'Unmarried'. We don't use the words 'Idiot' or 'Cripple' to describe people today.

In this Bird's Custard advert two chefs make custard, one using eggs and one using custard powder. The slogan reads: No Eggs! No Trouble! No Risk!

"WHAT, ANOTHER?"

BIRD'S CUSTARD POWDER makes Delicious Custard—a delightful accompaniment to every Sweet Dish, Pudding, or Stewed Fruit. An endless variety of choice Dishes can be made from the Recipes enclosed with each packet.
NO EGGS! NO TROUBLE! NO RISK!
N.B.—Ladies and housekeepers are told to their names a number of Dainty Dishes for the Dinner and Supper Table by consulting the handy little book entitled "PASTRY AND SWEETS." It will be forwarded, GRATIS and POST FREE, on receipt of address, by ALFRED BIRD and SONS, DEVONSHIRE WORKS, BIRMINGHAM.

Why do you think these two descriptions of Birmingham are so different?

How do we know?

Read these two accounts of Birmingham which were written 50 years apart. The first is a description from the travel writer George Borrow who visited Birmingham in 1854. The second account is an article from the Birmingham Daily Gazette by J. Cuming Walter, which was published in a book in 1901 called 'Scenes in Slum-land'.

At length we drew near the great workshop of England, called by some, Brummagem or Bromwicham, by others Birmingham. At Birmingham station I became a modern Englishman, proud of modern England's science and energy; that station alone is enough to make one proud, with its thousand trains dashing off in all directions. My modern English pride accompanied me all the way to Tipton; for all along the route there were wonderful evidences of English skill and enterprise; in chimneys high as cathedral spires, vomiting forth smoke, furnaces emitting flame and lava, and in the sound of gigantic hammers, wielded by steam, the Englishman's slave.

I am a modern Englishman!

A First Glance Round

The air is heavy with a sooty smoke, and here it is that the poor live – and wither away and die. How do they live? Look at the houses, the alleys, the courts, the ill-lit, ill-paved, walled-in squares, with last night's rain still trickling down from the roofs and making pools in the yards. Look at the begrimed windows, the broken glass, the [holes] stopped with yellow paper or filthy rags; glance in at the rooms where large families eat and sleep every day and every night, amid rags and vermin, within dank and mildewed walls. Here in the prison-like houses of the courts, many are herded together, and overcrowding is the rule, not the exception. The poor have nowhere else to go.

CELT   500 BC

ROMAN AD 43-410

ANGLO-SAXON AD 450-1066

VIKING AD 865-1066

MEDIEVAL TIMES
1066-1485

Health and Education

The Earl of Dartmouth turns the silver key and unlocks the ornate gates. 'Handsworth Park is open to the people for ever!' he declares. Crowds of people stream into the park. They gasp with delight at the lake, fountain and bandstand. Children run up onto the railway bridge to cheer as the trains cross the park below.

Aston Villa FC won the FA Cup in 1887. Team Captain Archie Hunter is holding the ball.

We won the Cup! We won the Cup!

Birmingham's drinking water takes two days to flow by gravity all the way from Wales.

Fresh Air and Clean Water

In 1853 an outbreak of cholera began in Birmingham. The disease was carried in the dirty drinking water and sewage in the streets. When Mayor Joseph Chamberlain took over in 1873, Birmingham Town Hall buzzed with plans for improvements. Chamberlain oversaw plans to pipe clean, fresh water 115 km from Wales to Birmingham. We still rely on the same drinking water system – not to mention the Victorian sewage system!

The Victorians opened new parks in Cannon Hill and Handsworth so that people could escape the smoky air of the city. The Victorians believed in healthy exercise. Aston Villa Football Club began in 1874 in the grounds of Aston Hall. Birmingham City FC and Warwickshire County Cricket Club at Edgbaston were founded soon after.

...1879 NEW CADBURY FACTORY OPENS...1898 HANDSWORTH PARK OPENS...

Cadbury

Some factory owners wanted their workers to live better, healthier lives. In 1879, George Cadbury moved his chocolate factory from Bridge Street to his new 'factory in a garden' at Bournville. The new factory had a canteen for the workers. Cadbury built new, roomy houses for the workers, with schools and sports fields. He even gave the Lickey Hills to the people of Birmingham in 1888. There were no pubs at Bournville because the Cadbury family were religious Quakers who didn't approve of alcohol.

Some factory owners, like George and Elizabeth Cadbury, believed in looking after their workers. They even built a special village for their workers.

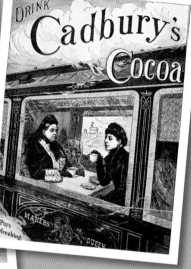

This advert shows Queen Victoria enjoying a cup of cocoa. Cadbury received a royal warrant in 1842.

Education for All

At the beginning of Queen Victoria's reign, only rich children went to school. But new laws said that all children should go to school, for free, at least until the age of 12. Over the next 20 years, 16 new Board Schools were built in Birmingham. Read this imaginary letter from 10-year-old Edward Nailor describing his new school.

31st day of March, 1875

My dear brother William

You will see from my letter that I have learned a great deal at school this year. There are more than 100 pupils in our class. We learn the '3Rs' - _reading, writing_ and _arithmetic_. I practise my writing on a slate. But our teacher is strict. Yesterday I was beaten with a cane, just for talking in class.

I know I am lucky to go to school every day, not just to Sunday School like you did. It has been hard without my wages. But I will be able to get a better job, because I can read and write.

I am proud of our school. It is a beautiful new building of red brick with a high bell tower. It is much warmer than home, too.

Your loving younger brother,

Edward Nailor

SPOT THIS!

Can you spot this bandstand in Handsworth Park? It was restored for the reopening of the park in 2006 - over 100 years after it was first built.

Birmingham at War

No streetlamps are lit. The city streets are dark as new blackout curtains are drawn tight. Indoors, tense and nervous, everyone listens to the news on the wireless. And then...the warning sirens. Quick! To the shelters! The moonlit skies overhead are full of circling black shadows, ready to drop their deadly bombs. Will they live to see the morning?

Stained-glass windows, designed by Edward Burne-Jones, were taken out of St Philip's Cathedral and kept in a safe place until the war was over.

Preparing for War

It was only 22 years since World War One had ended. In that war, Birmingham's factories had made rifles and bombs for British troops to use. Twelve thousand of Birmingham's young men died on the battlefields of France and Belgium.

Now again, in World War Two, young men were being sent away to fight. But this time, unlike World War One, the war came home to Birmingham. It was heavily bombed like London and Coventry. Many houses, factories and churches were destroyed or damaged.

Sandbags were piled up around the Town Hall in Birmingham to save the windows from being blown out.

...1939 WORLD WAR TWO DECLARED...1940 BATTLE OF BRITAIN...

TUDOR
1485-1603

STUART
1603-1714

GEORGIAN
1714-1837

VICTORIAN
1837-1901

MODERN
TIMES
1902-NOW

Birmingham Helps Win the War

Birmingham played a vital role in World War Two. Factories worked night and day to make aircraft, ammunition, bombs and mines. Eleven thousand Spitfire planes were made and flown from Castle Bromwich Aircraft Factory — half the number ever made. The speedy, agile Spitfires helped to win the Battle of Britain in 1940. The Birmingham Small Arms or BSA factory at Small Heath produced over two million rifles and machine guns.

The factories were desperate for workers, as men went away to fight. Women worked long hours in the factories, learning new skills and manufacturing planes and weapons. Free nurseries looked after the children while the women worked.

This Spitfire memorial sculpture near Castle Bromwich was designed by Tim Tolkien, the grandson of the author of Lord of the Rings.

The Birmingham Blitz

Birmingham's weapon factories made it a target for the German bombers. The night-time air raids of the Birmingham Blitz went on for nearly three years. Nowhere in the city was safe. Over 2,000 people died, and thousands more were made homeless. The German bombers hoped to shatter the Brummies' spirit. But bravely, the workers carried on.

Birmingham's worst air-raid disaster was one November night in 1940, when two bombs fell on the BSA factory at Small Heath. The fire brigade pumped water from the canal to put out the fire. Fifty-three night-shift workers were killed.

I'd better not drop this shell – the whole factory would explode!

Food was in short supply during the war. Everyone had a ration book to share food fairly.

ST THOMAS'S CHURCH
VICTIM OF WORLD WAR II

SPOT THIS!

Can you spot this plaque which remembers the victims of World War Two? St Thomas's Church was bombed, but part of it survived and the ruins have been turned into a peace garden.

CELT
500 BC

ROMAN
AD 43-410

ANGLO-
SAXON
AD 450-
1066

VIKING
AD 865-
1066

MEDIEVAL
TIMES
1066-
1485

On 31st August 1939 the first children were evacuated, or sent away from Birmingham. They were sent to the countryside, away from the Blitz. In this made-up letter, 11-year-old Elsie Smith writes back home to her mum after being evacuated with her brother, Jack.

I hope somebody nice and kind picks us.

Dear Mum and Dad,

Jack and I both cried after we said goodbye to you at New Street Station, but we soon started to enjoy the train journey. Everyone was singing, and pointing at the cows in the green fields!

We carried our suitcases and gas masks all the way from the station to the village hall – it felt like miles! A kind lady called Mrs Farmer took us in. Her son is a soldier away fighting in Europe, so we can sleep in his room. At first it felt strange, but now we are settling in.

Yesterday Jack and I helped Mrs Farmer dig a vegetable patch in the back garden. Tomorrow we will plant potatoes. Then we will have enough food to eat during the war. She said we were digging for victory!

I hope you and Dad will stay safe. We listen to the news on the wireless to hear if there have been any bombs in Brum.

Oh Mum, we miss you at bedtime, our Jack and me. But we try to be brave, just like our soldiers overseas.

Love from your Elsie

TUDOR
1485-1603

STUART
1603-1714

GEORGIAN
1714-1837

VICTORIAN
1837-1901

MODERN
TIMES
1902-NOW

Peep!
Air-raid warden here!
Take cover!
Take cover!

I'd better pitch
in if we're going
to win!

TAKE
COVER

How do we know?

Thousands of documents from World War Two
have survived, giving us an idea of what it
was like to live through the war. As ships
bringing food from abroad were blockaded by
German U-boats, people were encouraged to
grow more food. Girls from the towns were
sent to the countryside as part of the Women's
Land Army. In the towns, the men who were
left behind took up duties such as air-raid
wardens, fire fighters and the home guard.
Read this notice about a Smoke Practice:

DIG FOR
VICTORY

Government leaflets
asked people to turn their
parks and gardens into
vegetable plots.

IMPORTANT NOTICE.

SMOKE PRACTICE.

A corrugated iron hut has been erected on the waste ground
adjacent to the Royalty Cinema, Harborne, for practice by
this Sub-Division. The general idea is for waste materials
of any kind to be set alight inside this hut and a dummy
figure placed within which is rescued by the Fire Guards
crawling into the hut, SWARF IS NOT TO BE USED.

Sgt: Fox will be present at all exercises
and will bring with him an incendiary bomb to give added
interest to the operations.

I am asked to make arrangements for personnel
to take part in this very necessary practice which will
be held at 10.30 a.m. JULY. 18th.1943. (Sunday)

N.B.

PLEASE NOTE THAT THIS PRACTICE IS COMPULSORY AND I
AGAIN POINT OUT THE NECESSITY OF ATTENDANCE.

Signed,
Senior Fire Guard

16-6-43.

23

CELT
500 BC

ROMAN
AD 43-410

ANGLO-
SAXON
AD 450-
1066

VIKING
AD 865-
1066

MEDIEVAL
TIMES
1066-
1485

Rebuilding Birmingham

'Welcome to our brand new streets in the sky!' says the mayor. These bright, new tower blocks are a fresh start. The windows look out over green fields beyond the city. Every flat has a modern kitchen, bathroom and indoor toilet – and all as clean as a new pin. Families cheer as they unlock their new front doors.

New Homes

Over 12,000 homes had been destroyed in the Birmingham Blitz. After World War Two, people wanted to make a new, better life. It was time to rebuild Birmingham.

The council knocked down masses of dreadful slum houses. In their place, they built bright new houses, flats and tower blocks all over Birmingham. Castle Vale's 5,000 homes sprang up on the Castle Bromwich airfield. New homes were built on the city's green outskirts, like Kings Norton's Three Estates.

At first the new residents loved these modern homes. They were glad to leave behind their damp, cramped old houses... and most of all, the outside loos! But people started to miss their old streets and communities. Some estates grew run-down and unpopular.

Spaghetti Junction - real name Gravelly Hill Interchange - joins two roads with the M6 motorway.

Spaghetti Junction crosses two rivers, three canals and two railway lines.

TUDOR 1485-1603	STUART 1603-1714	GEORGIAN 1714-1837	VICTORIAN 1837-1901	MODERN TIMES 1902-NOW

Improvements?

In the 1970s the council started to improve existing houses instead of knocking them down. Then people could stay in their homes, and communities could stay together.

Birmingham, centre of the motor industry, was in love with cars. Ring-roads were built circling Birmingham. Spaghetti Junction linked the city with the new motorways. This was good for drivers... but not so good for pedestrians, who had to walk through subways to get around the city.

Jamaican men on board the Empire Windrush read the newspaper looking for jobs and a place to live.

New Arrivals

Britain needed more workers. People from the old colonies were invited to come to work and live in Britain. Many people settled in Birmingham from India, Pakistan and the Caribbean. They followed in the footsteps of earlier Jewish and Irish immigrants, who by now formed settled communities.

The new arrivals worked in hospitals, on buses and trains, and in the factories. Many faced racial prejudice. Often they were turned down for jobs or housing. But they stayed and worked hard. Many sent money to relatives who had stayed back home. Soon Afro-Caribbean and Asian communities put down roots.

The population of Birmingham was higher in 1951 than it is today!

How do we know?

A ship called the Empire Windrush arrived in London on 22nd June 1948 bringing 492 hopeful immigrants from Jamaica. Many Jamaicans moved to Birmingham where there was work. But they did not always receive the warm welcome they expected. Newspapers record the attitudes of the time.

SPOT THIS!

Many unloved buildings from the 1960s and 1970s have already been demolished. But the Rotunda is still standing. Can you spot it?

CELT
500 BC

ROMAN
AD 43-410

ANGLO-
SAXON
AD 450-
1066

VIKING
AD 865-
1066

MEDIEVAL
TIMES
1066-
1485

City of Cars

The Birmingham Small Arms Company, the Wolseley Sheep Shearing Company, Alldays and Onions Pneumatic Engineering, Lanchester Engine Company: who would have thought that companies with names like this would become part of one of the major car manufacturing cities in the world?

From Bikes to Motors

The Birmingham Small Arms Company (BSA) was founded by 14 gunsmiths in 1861. Based in the Gun Quarter, it supplied guns for the Crimean War. By the 1880s, BSA was also making bicycles. By the 1920s it was producing motorcycles and Daimler cars.

Herbert Austin worked for the Wolseley Sheep Shearing Company, which made a mechanical sheep-shearer, tools and motors. He left in 1905 to set up his own company called the Austin Motor Company in an old print works in Longbridge.

The Austin Seven Famous all ov...

THE NEW RUBY Saloon

Smarter than ever, the "New Ruby" saloon, with Pytchley sliding roof or fixed head, appeals to all who wish for de luxe travel with maximum economy. With attractive new body lines and improved mechanical features, it will make a still wider appeal. With accommodation for four, upholstery is in best quality leather with pneumatic seats for each person. The quarter windows wind open and direction indicators have automatic re-turn. Front seats are instantly adjustable over a wide range.

£125 PRICE AT WORKS
THE FIXED HEAD SALOON IS £118

THE PEARL...

THE NIPPY Sports
The "Nippy" is just the car for the modern youth and his lady. Its light and low-built body is extremely comfortable under all conditions, and luggage can be stowed in the tail.
With standard engine **£130** With specially tuned engine **£142**
PRICES AT WORKS

THE TWO-SEATER

The Two-Seater is a handy little runabout with enclosed luggage accommodation, and an easily operated hood.
Side screens can be folded or carried in the thickness of the doors. A cover is provided for the spare wheel, and the independent front seats are adjustable. **£102-10** PRICE AT WORKS

THE AUSTIN

THE O...

"Covers the Country!"

By 1959, BMC at Longbridge was making the new popular mini car on an assembly line.

In the 1930s Austin was making several car models: the Ruby Saloon, the Pearl Cabriolet, the Nippy Sports, the Two-Seater and the Open Road Tourer. Well-off people could buy one for between £102 and £142.

Three Lanchester brothers built the first British petrol-driven car in 1895. It was steered using a boat's tiller.

Alldays and Onions was an old blacksmith company specialising in making bellows. Their first cars included a quadricycle and one model that had the steering wheel in the back seat!

TUDOR
1485-1603

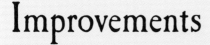

STUART
1603-1714

GEORGIAN
1714-1837

VICTORIAN
1837-1901

MODERN
TIMES
1902-NOW

Improvements

Before World War One, car drivers had to reach out of the car to work the windscreen wipers. In 1917 an electric motor was introduced to do the work. The Dunlop Pneumatic Tyre Company moved to Birmingham in 1918, building a new factory called Fort Dunlop. Its air-filled tyres made car journeys smoother. During World War Two, Birmingham's factories were busy making munitions, tanks and aeroplanes. It wasn't until after the war that they began making newer and better cars. Drivers had to wait until the 1960s to have wind-down windows.

The record number of people who can fit into a mini at the same time is 39!

A New Generation

By the 1950s many of the small car companies had joined together to make bigger vehicle manufacturers. Austin, Morris, MG, Riley and Wolseley came together in 1952 to become the British Motor Corporation (BMC). By 1968 it had become British Leyland.

Birmingham was such a big centre for car manufacturing that The Motor Show moved from London to the NEC in 1978.

Today Jaguar Land Rover is using aluminium and modern engine technology to make more fuel-efficient cars.

SPOT THIS!

Can you spot this Jaguar car mascot outside the West Bromwich assembly plant? You might spot them on car bonnets too!

There are lots of cycle paths around Birmingham today.

The Jaguar Land Rover factory at Solihull uses fully automated robots on the production line.

Birmingham Today and Tomorrow...

Today, Birmingham is Britain's second biggest city, rich with history and modern, global links. People from many cultures live side by side. Brummies worship in mosques, synagogues, gurdwaras and Buddhist temples, as well as historic churches like St Martin's. Restaurants serve dishes from all over the world – not to mention the famous Birmingham balti.

The Mailbox, opened in 2000, is full of smart shops and restaurants. The building used to be the Royal Mail sorting office – that's how it got its name.

Birmingham's Zero Carbon House leads plans to transform the city's older houses into eco-homes to tackle climate change.

Birmingham now has four universities educating young people for the future. Colleges such as Matthew Boulton, Joseph Chamberlain and Cadbury College keep alive great names from our city's past.

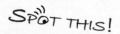

SPOT THIS!

Can you spot this statue of Queen Victoria? Clue: a square is named after her.

...2000 MAILBOX OPENS...

There are around 50 different home languages spoken by children in Birmingham's schools.

Aston Villa FC, Birmingham City FC and Warwickshire County Cricket Club at Edgbaston are well into their second century.

Birmingham's sports teams are famous around the world!

Birmingham is full of contrasts. The Selfridges building looks modern next to the spire of St Martin's.

Birmingham's Central Mosque was built in 1969, the second mosque built in Britain. It can hold 3,000 worshippers.

How will they know?

Today's technology may mean that written records are replaced with emails, music, even Facebook postings. Tourists take photos and souvenirs back to their homes for future generations to see. Rubbish tips could give us an insight into what people use and throw out. What will remain for historians in the future to find out about 21st-century Birmingham?

Come and find me in the Bull Ring and pat me – if you dare!

The bronze bull statue was designed by Laurence Broderick.

Glossary

AD – a short way of writing the Latin words anno Domini, which mean 'in the year of our Lord', i.e. after the birth of Christ.

Anvil – a base of solid steel that a blacksmith uses to hammer hot metal on.

Bellows – two-handled leather bag that pumps out air to feed oxygen to the flames of a fire.

Blackout curtains – heavy black curtains that stop light from windows being visible to enemy aircraft.

Blitz – when the Germans bombed towns during World War Two, it was called the Blitz.

Blockade – to prevent a country getting food or aid by blocking its roads or seas.

Catholic – a member of the Christian religion that considers the Pope the head of its Church.

Census – an official count of a population and who is in it.

Cholera – a deadly disease caused by filthy water.

Christianity – a religion whose followers believe Christ is the son of God.

Domesday Book – William the Conqueror's men recorded how much land and wealth was in the kingdom, and who owned it. The results were written in the Domesday Book.

Evacuate – having to leave your home and live somewhere else for safety.

Garrison – where soldiers stay while guarding a place.

Gas mask – used in World War Two, this mask provented you from breathing poisonous gas.

Gurdwara – where people of the Sikh religion go to worship.

Home Guard – volunteers who wanted to help protect Britain during World War Two.

Munitions – another word for military stores, especially one that holds ammunition.

Musket – a long-barrelled gun, loaded from the front, used from the 16th to the 18th centuries.

Musketeer – a soldier armed with a matchlock musket.

Pagan – someone who believes in more than one god.

Parliamentarian – anyone who fought on Oliver Cromwell's side in the English Civil War.

Ration book – during World War Two, certain food was scarce and had to be rationed. Your ration book showed how much of this food you could have every week. Once you'd used it up, you wouldn't get any more until the next week.

Royalist – anyone who fought on the side of King Charles I in the English Civil War.

Royal Charter – written permission from the king or queen to do something.

Sirens – during World War Two enemy planes dropped bombs on Britain. This was called an air raid. Loud air-raid sirens warned people that planes were coming.

Slave trade – making money by buying and selling people as slaves. Slaves have no freedom or rights, and work for no payment.

Slum – a very poor part of a city that's rundown, dirty and usually overcrowded with people.

Swarf – small pieces of waste metal.

Workhouse – where poor people lived and worked when they had nowhere else to go.

Index

Acknowledgements

The author and publishers would like to thank the following people for their generous help:

Wendy Carter from the Harborne Library and the family of Don Wright.
William Dargue's *History of Birmingham on your Doorstep*, which is freely available
on the Birmingham Grid for Learning at www.bgfl.org

The publishers would like to thank the following people and organisations
for their permission to reproduce material on the following pages:

p5: Phil Champion; p7: Marco Secchi/Alamy; p10: Martin Bennett/Alamy; p13: Pictorial Press Ltd/Alamy;
p15: Peter Higginbotham Collection/Mary Evans; p17: Mary Evans Picture Library; p18: Courtesy Aston Villa FC;
p19: History Archive/Alamy, Pictorial Press Ltd/Alamy; p20: Tupungato/Shutterstock, Trinity Mirror/Mirrorpix/Alamy;
p23: Robert Hunt Library/Mary Evans, text reproduced from the Don Wright collection held at the Harborne Library
with kind permission from the Wright family; p24: David Bagnall/Alamy; p25: Illustrated London News Ltd/Mary Evans,
www.photoeverywhere.co.uk; p26: Mary Evans Picture Library/Alamy, Trinity Mirror/ Mirrorpix/Alamy;
p27: Images of Birmingham Premium/Alamy; p29 esp_imaging/istock.

All other images copyright of Hometown World

Written by Mandy Ross
Educational consultant: Neil Thompson
Local history consultants: Malcolm Dick
Designed by Stephen Prosser

Illustrated by Kate Davies, Dynamo Ltd, Virginia Gray, Peter Kent,
John MacGregor, Victor McLindon and Tim Sutcliffe.
Additional photographs by Alex Long

This edition published by HOMETOWN WORLD in 2011
Hometown World Ltd
7 Northumberland Buildings
Bath BA1 2JB

www.hometownworld.co.uk